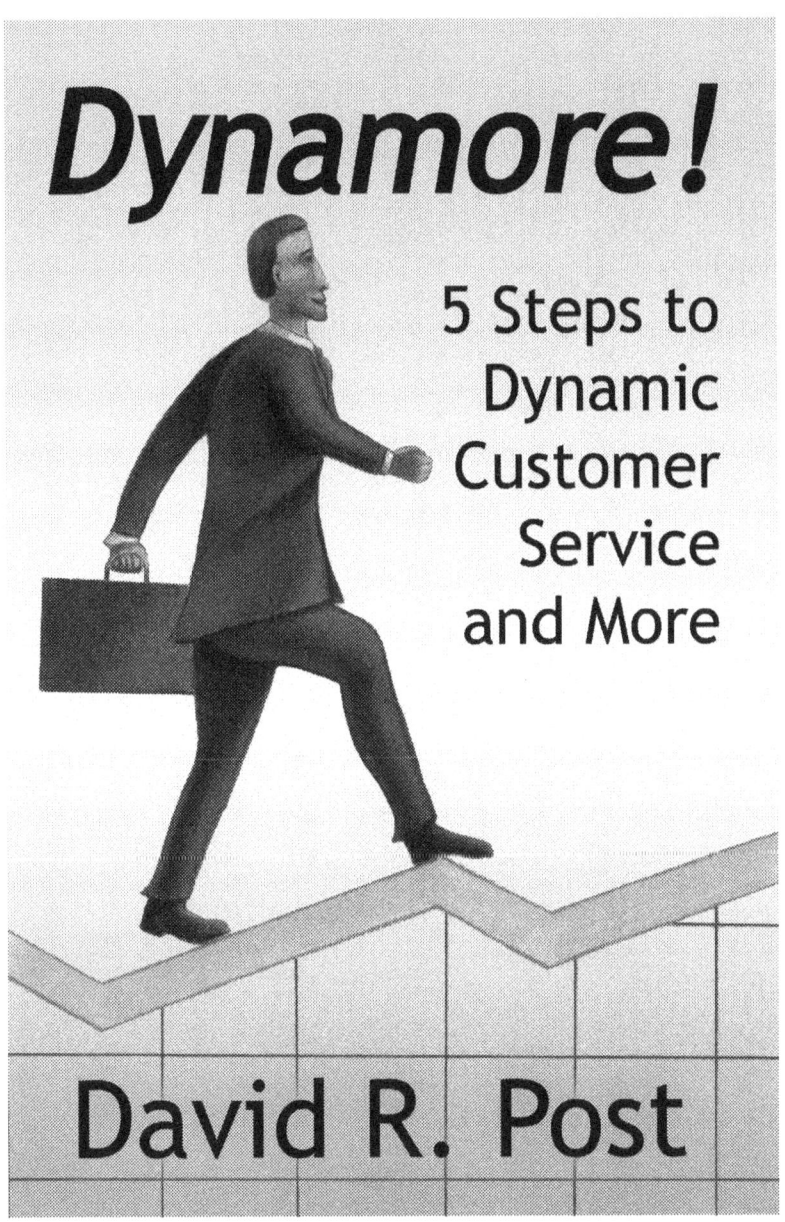

# Dynamore!

## 5 Steps to Dynamic Customer Service and More

# David R. Post

Bloomington, IN          authorHOUSE™          Milton Keynes, UK

*AuthorHouse™*
*1663 Liberty Drive, Suite 200*
*Bloomington, IN 47403*
*www.authorhouse.com*
*Phone: 1-800-839-8640*

*AuthorHouse™ UK Ltd.*
*500 Avebury Boulevard*
*Central Milton Keynes, MK9 2BE*
*www.authorhouse.co.uk*
*Phone: 08001974150*

*First published by AuthorHouse 12/13/2006*

*ISBN: 1-4259-3611-3 (e)*
*ISBN: 1-4259-3610-5 (sc)*

*Printed in the United States of America*
*Bloomington, Indiana*

*This book is printed on acid-free paper.*

I am dedicating my first book, **DYNAMORE! 5 Steps to Dynamic Customer Service and More**, to my wife and life partner Launa Haney Post.  She has been there for me in everything I have attempted and accomplished.  She has taught me a great deal about customer service, consumer advocacy, and about how to treat people. She has also been my coach, partner, guidance counselor, teammate, and always my best friend!  Thanks Launa!

What is customer service and what does it mean to you and your company? When was the last time you truly received outstanding customer service and how did it make you feel? Are you providing Dynamic Customer Service?

Customer service has become a lost art in our society. What once was expected on a daily basis is now a scarce commodity. Somewhere over the last few years during our changing business environment we have lost the concept of providing quality customer service. You will hear people speak of it yet you don't usually stumble on to it. When I was growing up we still had "*full service*" everything and people took real pride in their company and the service they had to offer. Somehow, someway we have dropped the "*customer service*" ball.

My wife and I actually travel great distances on a regular basis to buy our goods and spend our money solely based on the fact that we always receive top of the line customer service. The people we meet and deal with are almost always very helpful and very friendly. We have also noticed that most of the customer service people we meet have a good understanding of their company and the products and services they offer.

For example, I remember this young gentlemen going above and beyond the call of duty in showing me a little about car stereos. He went out of his way to tell me the positives and negatives of each unit. This Customer Service Rep steered me away from the units that have had problems even though they probably would have made him the most money based on the cost. He directed me to a less expensive unit that had a better performance record. This young man must have spent twenty plus minutes with me and I didn't even buy the thing but guess where I will be going when I make the decision!

It is critical for any and all companies and customer service teams to get back to the basic and sound fundamentals of proactive, knowledgeable, and pleasant service. Some people think that customer service is no big deal but it is probably the most important element a company can provide.

This book focuses on implementing some very basic fundamentals that will help improve your customer service performance either as an individual or as a company. Though the book focuses on Customer Service Representatives or Inside Sales People, the concepts apply to anyone who deals with customers or the public in general. That basically means everyone. Don't forget we are all in some way a customer service person just as we are all salespeople. No matter what your occupation or responsibility you are selling and servicing in some way, shape, of form. These steps apply to both male and female customer service individuals but for the sake of simplicity I will be referring to "he" and "him" as customers or Customer Service/Sales Reps. After reading and practicing these concepts you will be able to implement the steps into your everyday customer approach.

The concepts in this book come from a lifetime of customer service work in a number of professional areas and I believe you will find they address your particular customer service environment. Please read, understand, and implement the following easy steps to customer service excellence. I think you will find this book to be an easy and enjoyable read. I hope the concepts have the same effect on your career or company that they have had on mine. In the retail game, Investment business, and the Industrial business sector, there are five basic customer steps to achieving Dynamic Customer Service and more. These five steps have always propelled me to the top of my game and have laid the groundwork for financial gain, career growth and self-satisfaction. *I have based my business career and much of my daily life activity on following these steps.*

# DYNAMORE!
## 5 Steps to Dynamic Customer Service and More

**By David R. Post**

Remember the last time you tried to get help or an answer from a particular company and made absolutely no progress at all. In fact the Customer Service Rep actually seemed bent out of shape because you needed your answer right away. There was no real extra effort to get your answer or solve your problem. It was no big deal to this Customer Service person. He really didn't seem interested or concerned with your needs. This is what I jokingly refer to as *"service with a snarl."* When you encounter this type of service you will recognize it immediately and it will most likely stay with you for some time. This is not what I consider customer service.

Customer service is one of the most critical factors in making a business successful in today's market. In fact it may very well be the most important factor in whether or not a customer seeks to do business with you. In today's competitive business environment most companies are going to represent a pretty good product. Most companies also realize that *"just in time delivery*" (being able to attain product just in time to install and start things up or finish a project at the last minute) is essential since the days of companies carrying lots of stock and inventory are over.

In light of this, the promise of "*just in time delivery*" must be fulfilled. Most companies will be as competitive as possible with their pricing. With most companies covering all the bases with good product, competitive pricing and timely delivery, what makes the difference in the competition? **CUSTOMER SERVICE**! Let's look at a scenario. You frequent two different retail outlets for your shopping needs. Both stores have quality merchandise, diversified selections, and reasonably competitive pricing. The difference is at one location you receive top of the line service and attention whereas the other store doesn't seem to know you exist. Where do you make your buys? Customer Service makes the difference!

What is **customer service**? As you move through this book and follow the five easy steps I believe the true meaning of customer service will be put into perspective. You will also develop a good understanding of and enthusiasm for genuinely helping your customers. When you have finished this easy five-step process you will have the knowledge, understanding, and the action plan to implement your new customer service approach. This will positively impact your customer base, your company, and you.

The following steps will show you a very easy and effective method of achieving Dynamic Customer Service and more. These ideas aren't based on scientific experiments or laboratory tests but instead come from over twenty years of customer service experience, learning from mistakes, and building relationships with customers and customer service teams. I have been called a *"Customer Service Guru."* I hope that's true. I know I have devoted my time in all facets of my career to providing quality customer service. I have learned vast and varied concepts and approaches in dealing with customer service in every position I have held in Retail, the Investment Business, and Industrial Distribution Sales.

I know in my heart if you apply the following concepts and implement the dynamic five steps in this book you and your company will *"Raise the Level"* of the customer service you provide and enhance your business efforts in efficiency, sales, and profitability. This will mean better service to your

*David R. Post*

customers, more sales for your company, and most of all enhanced performance and opportunities for you!

# Dynamic Step 1: Do what you say you are going to do

This first step is one of the most crucial in developing a solid working relationship with your customer. By doing this you will gain both trust and confidence from your customer. Many customer service teams drop the ball here by not being proactive when it comes to expediting, getting answers, or having to deliver bad news to a customer. Put yourself in the customer's shoes and imagine what you would be looking for with customer service satisfaction! Remember what you desire in customer service from others and go out of your way to put forth that effort for your customers.

If you tell a customer you are going to do something you better very well do it. Even if the information is not exactly what the customer wants to hear, you have to get back to him with an answer. For example, if you tell a customer that you will have an answer by five o'clock that day it is essential that you touch base with him by five o'clock! This timely response is critical. Get back to your customer! If you promise to look something up or check out a scenario for your customer once again get back to him in a timely fashion.

Even if you don't have the answer yet because your supplier has not given you the final answer or you are still expediting the situation, just call the customer and give them an update. ***Stay true to your word and keep your commitment.*** Your customer will appreciate your efforts, honesty, and integrity. There is no better way to build your customer relationships and keep the customers coming back to you. Responding to your customers in a timely manner will have a major impact in how they view your service and your company.

Please don't try to commit this follow-up to memory. We will discuss this in the next chapter but please put follow-up calls in your planner, in your CRM (customer relations management) program or in your daily desktop to-do list. If you use these tools correctly you will not miss a good follow-up opportunity. These follow-up calls can lead to add on or future business. This is imperative to success and will take you to a higher customer service level.

**Example: "Mr. Customer, I told you I would get back to you with an answer today. I don't have the final numbers yet but I am pulling out all the stops and jumping through hoops and I will get it done. I wanted to let you know I'm**

**on top of it and I will have it ready for you first thing in the morning."**

Now, we did not exactly have the right answer for the customer but we let him know we were on top of things and that we would get the job done. What signal do we send if we don't call the customer back with an update? How does that make him feel? How does he prepare without his answers? On the other hand how does he feel when you respond exactly as you said you would?

Recently I had asked a CSR from a vendor of ours to help me identify a part number that I didn't recognize. He said he would call me back in fifteen minutes. Right at the fifteen-minute mark he called me back. Even though he could not identify the part it meant a lot to me that he put forth the effort and followed through. He kept his commitment! By doing what he said he was going to do he has strengthened my trust and confidence in him. I will call upon him again.

This is a key element in customer service success. Put yourself in the customer's shoes. Would you rather hear from your supplier with an update even if its bad news so you might be able to make other arrangements or prepare correctly or would you prefer to not here anything at all until its too late to make adjustments. This is the difference between being proactive and using the "***bury your head in the sand***" routine. Keep in mind the old "***no news is good news***" saying is a fallacy in today's business world. The customer has to know what is going on at all times. ***They want to know and they need to know.*** This proactive approach is a key element to your future success no matter what area of customer service you provide.

Here is another example: My wife planned a recent trip with a group of people to visit a local bee farm. She thought this would be something different to do. She was able to get her hands on a flier about the farm but it didn't have any business hours stated. That was their first mistake.

She called to attain the hours and left an appropriate voice mail. Days later there was no response. Being the consumer advocate she is she followed up with another phone call to see what was going on. She finally reached someone and he told her that they were remodeling and didn't know when they would re-open. ***Enough said***!

Obviously that was the end of that trip and who knows how much money the business lost from that group or other groups. All it would have taken was the appropriate business voice mail or a return call giving her a heads up. A response of any fashion would have most likely brought the group to the farm with money in hand!

When the customer calls us with a question or problem he wants to know two things. One, that someone is on top of his situation and two that everything is all right and somehow, someway they will meet his goal! If we satisfy these two needs we will have a loyal customer.

This concept is the same internally within your own team, company, etc. If you tell an employee or a team member that you are going to do something, then do it. This will set a good example and precedent among your team. Imagine if you tell an employee that you will have his review in the near future and then never do it. What kind of impact does that have on him? What if you tell him you will look into a certain problem or situation and then you don't get around to it. What will his trust level be in the future? But what happens when you do keep your commitments and follow-through completely?  How is his attitude and what is his trust level now?  I have spent my career trying everything humanly possible to give quick responses and solutions to my customers, teammates, and employees. It has had a positive impact on my customer relationships and my team building success.

A good concept to keep in mind is to treat your co-workers, team members, and employees the same way you want to be treated and the same way you treat your customers.  In essence, they are your internal customers.  By staying true to your word you will build trust and confidence within your team and among your co-workers.

This first step is essential in building dynamic relationships with your customers, both internal and external, and critical to developing your own customer service expertise.  I have learned many lessons over the years about getting back to the customer with good news or bad and this approach will put you a step ahead of the competition.  From calling a customer to let him know his suit is going on sale to letting a client know the stock market was struggling but to sit tight and ride it out to getting back to a customer to advise that his emergency part was shipping priority overnight, I always followed up and that gave me the edge. If you commit to something then find a way to make it happen. This is the first step in achieving Dynamic Customer Service. Remember Dynamic Step 1 and keep your commitments and stay true to your word. ***Do what you say you are going to do!***

# Dynamic Step 2: Time Management and Organization
## (Manage your time; don't let time manage you!)

Another key dynamic step in being at the top of your game in customer service is the combination of time management and organization. Remember this phrase for the rest of your life: "*Organization and time management are the keys to business life*." These words will have true meaning as we work our way through this chapter.

The pace of a customer service team or customer service center is hectic, chaotic, and at times can easily get out of control. It is very easy for a CSR or Inside Salesperson to get swallowed up by this environment. In fact, most customer service positions are very demanding and call for the ability to multi-task and juggle many responsibilities. The most effective customer service experts are very proficient at staying organized and managing their time. Remember, the CSR who can **organize**, **prioritize**, and **manage time** efficiently will be successful.

I once had to choose between two candidates for a promotion to fill a management position. Both candidates had good qualities and strengths in different areas. In fact, they were very close in attributes and talent. The candidate I chose was the one who could organize, manage their time efficiently, and make the extra things happen. I felt this person's organization and time management skills would help them develop into an efficient and successful manager.

There are two essentials to effective time management. The first is to always arrive at work with your action plan for the day. What I mean by this is that you need to start everyday with a very aggressive schedule of items or tasks that must be accomplished by the time you finish your day. You can accomplish this a number of ways. You can use a daily planner, desktop planner, clipboard task list or your daily to-do task list in your laptop notebook or PC. The type of method is your choice. The critical factor is that you have a plan to implement daily.

There is a very important saying that floats around in the business sector that states, *"people don't plan to fail, they fail to plan."* There is a lot of truth to this saying. Nobody gets up in the morning and starts their day by saying, " I hope this is a totally confusing, disorganized and out of control type of day in which I get absolutely nothing accomplished." Most people simply fail to plan their work and/or fail to work their plan.

If you fall into this category and fail to plan your day then your efforts can and most likely will seem out of control and ineffective. When you find yourself shuffling from pile to pile you know you are in trouble. If you walk away from your desk to take care of something and upon returning you haven't a clue where to begin again, then you are in desperate need of organization. Step back, get organized and stick to your daily plan for greater success. **Once again plan your work and work your plan.**

Probably the best way to plan your day is to set it up the day before. When you are wrapping things up for the day take a couple of minutes to jot down or enter into your personal computer all the tasks you need to accomplish the next day. By doing this you will remember things because they are fresh in your mind and you will be ready to go first thing in the morning. Otherwise you may arrive at work the next day, look at your desk and say, " where in the heck do I even begin"?

***Once again, "Organization and time management are the keys to business life.*** " Here is an example of a dynamic daily attack plan right out of my planner:

| | |
|---|---|
| **7:30AM** | **Review Current Sales Numbers** |
| **8:00AM** | **Run Inventory Purchasing Report** |
| **8:30AM** | **Follow-up on pending Repair Project** |
| **9:00AM** | **develop new Systems Division Report** |
| **9:30AM** | **call new CRM Vendor for information** |
| **10:00AM** | **Prepare for Board Meeting** |
| **11:00AM** | **Meet with IT Department** |
| **12:00PM** | **Bank and Gas Errands during lunch** |
| **1:00PM** | **Work on New Training Program** |
| **3:00PM** | **Meet with Technical Support Department** |
| **4:00PM** | **Work on Demo Inventory Procedure** |
| **4:50PM** | **Set-up Action Plan for Friday** |
| **5:30PM** | **Pick-up pizza on trip home** |

This is a typical plan that I follow religiously and it is the only way I can stay organized and focused. I live and die by my daily plan. By having a proactive attack plan you will have a good starting point and the feeling of control and opportunity for accomplishment. Sometimes I will notice piles of work stacked up on a team member's desk. Some people think this is a sign of a busy person. Most likely this is a sign of a disorganized person who may be struggling with his workload and is not getting much accomplished.

When you start seeing "***piles***" on your desk you know you need an organizational upgrade. Follow this attack plan. 1. Sort the work into the appropriate categories such as orders to be entered, quotations, expediting, miscellaneous follow-up, filing, etc. 2. Prioritize the categories by importance and urgency factor (we will discuss this element in an upcoming paragraph). 3. Organize the categories into a bin system of some type and label accordingly. 4. Put these items into your daily attack plan that we have just discussed.

You will find by organizing the "***piles***" of work into an efficient attack system you will be more prepared to work through the tasks and clean-up any backlog. Some people believe a clean desk is a sign of not enough work or responsibility. I believe a clean desk and organized work area is a sign of an efficient and effective worker with solid time management skills.

There are two fun tests that I use as an example during my Customer Service Presentations that are good indicators of taking organization to the extreme. 1. Take out your wallet and look at the way your money is organized. If you have all bills heads up and facing front with largest denominations first, you might be on your way to organizational extreme. ***GREAT!***

2. Take out your key ring and look at your keys. If all the teeth face the same direction you are most likely an organizational maniac. **FANTASTIC!** All kidding aside, **"Organization and time management are the keys to business life."**

When you start each day you will have a list of things (like the one previously shown) that you need to attack. Now we all know that emergencies are going to come up, situations are going to arise, other people will need your help, and many other distractions may occur. You will need to take care of these in order of priority and then get immediately back to your daily action plan.

**For example**: You are working your action plan and you get an emergency call concerning a critical shipment that is lost somewhere. Obviously, you need to expedite and track this down and then get back to the customer as soon as possible with the information. Once you have accomplished this task you should go right back to your action plan and pick up where you left off.

This is where a lot of customer service and sales people drop the ball. Because so many situations do come up during the day most people tend to get totally off base after taking care of the emergencies, etc. and since they do not have a plan to resume, they have a very hard time re-focusing. Without a solid game plan to follow throughout the day chances of accomplishment are slim to none. This is why having an effective action plan is so critical.

When you do have a good common sense attack plan to follow everyday you will find yourself accomplishing so much more that your confidence will grow and you will feel better about tackling the next day's events. If you're operating an effective daily game plan then all the items on your list should be crossed off by the end of the day. If you cannot accomplish all the tasks then the remaining items must go on the very next day's plan, preferably at the top.

Let us look at two team members as an example. **Team Member number 1**. This team member is shuffling the "*piles*" throughout the day without any organized action plan. At the end of the day he leaves the "*piles*" where they are and bolts for the door at 5:00PM without any thought on tomorrow morning.

**Team Member number 2**. This team member is following his daily action plan checking off the items one by one and at the end of the day he neatly organizes paperwork into the appropriate work bin and fills out tomorrow morning's action plan starting with where he left off. His desk is clean and organized. Which team member will feel better about his accomplishments at the end of the day? Which team member will feel better about starting out the next day? Which team member will be set-up to have a productive workday? Which team member will most likely be successful?

Someone once told me that you should leave your desk and work area each night as if you were going on vacation and would not be back for a week. *GOOD ADVICE!* This means that when you leave work for the day your tasks are accomplished, your desk and work area are neat and organized, and your action plan is set for the next day.

As you get used to using this proactive method of time management you can take it to the next level. Instead of planning day to day you end up putting together a solid plan for the next two or three days, next week, or the next couple of weeks. When you have changes in your schedule you simply make the adjustments in your task list or attack plan. Remember to follow your list and use it effectively. **Some people try to rely strictly on memory and this is a definite recipe for failure**. It is nearly impossible to remember all tasks and follow-up items in today's hectic and ever changing business climate.

**For example**: A co-worker asked me if I could help him create a new report that would help analyze his division of the business. He wasn't in a great rush but I immediately put into my daily action plan and kept it on my list until it was completed. My teammate appreciated my efforts and I felt good about helping him with his project. I used my action plan to follow up and complete this task. **Do not try to commit to memory. Use your action plan**.

**The second important element of effective time management and organization is the ability to juggle and prioritize tasks**. This talent comes from a lot of hard work and experience. We all realize that in today's business sector it is critical that we are able to wear many hats and cover a great deal of territory. In other words we must be able to multi-task. Businesses are looking to reduce workforces and streamline the overall business flow to "*put more*" to bottom line profitability. Because of this approach the "*top of the line*" CSR or Salesperson must become more efficient, proactive and take on more responsibility. This will ultimately go to your bottom line as your company does performance evaluations, merit reviews etc. You can only gain from this approach. **Learn to prioritize and juggle tasks**!

To do this we need to always stay focused on moving ahead and growing our business. We can do this by periodically pausing and thinking to ourselves," is what I am doing right now critical or important to my business plan?"

How do you prioritize all the tasks, issues, and projects that need to be addressed during your workday? The most effective method is to categorize the tasks by level of importance and time sensitivity.

Most people will naturally prioritize the critical and urgent tasks first. This is just basic common sense. They are very critical and have immediate dead lines. The tricky part is what to prioritize next. Some people tend to migrate to what seems to be an urgent task but in reality doesn't carry a lot of value to your customer or your company. The most effective customer service person will instead prioritize those items that may not seem as urgent but are very important to your customer and your company. He realizes that these are important projects and the deadlines will come quickly. He doesn't want to be scrambling around at the last minute trying to "wing" a very important project.

I have always been careful to plan and prioritize this way since much of my business has been associated with project type responsibilities. Tasks that are in the future must be addressed and planned out in advance to be successful. If you wait until the last minute your end result may not be what you want or need.

**The following is a typical daily priority example:**

We have the following tasks on our daily action plan. How do we prioritize and attack the following items?

Number 1 is a $10,000 rush shipment that has to be on site the next day to get our best customer out of a jam and back in production. We know this is critical to the customer's end goal.

Number 2 is a customer that needs a .98 special gasket that you would have to spend several hours trying to locate. This is not a normal product we carry or for which we have easy availability.

Number 3 is a major customer project bid worth $50,000 that isn't due until four weeks from now. This is a project we really need to boost our current business and to solidify our relationship with this high potential customer.

Number 4 is a $50 customer return in which we sent the customer the correct replacement material and now we have to do the internal credit. The customer seems in no rush but we realize we have to issue credit to get this off his books.

What is our attack plan? We will take of care the rush shipment **(number 1)** and ship it out the door so we can get our customer back up and running. It is critical to the customer's situation and for our future business relationship to make this happen. We will then work on the big project bid **(number 3)** since it is of great value to the company and we know the deadline will sneak up on us. By attacking this project early and getting ahead of the game we will be prepared with an accurate and efficient quotation come bid deadline. We will spend little time on the gasket **(number 2)** since we don't really have a source for it and we will let the customer know quickly if we cannot locate the material **(Step 1)**. This will help us prioritize and our customer move on to another option if necessary. We will move onto the next task and we have been responsive and honest with our customer. Finally we will finish up the customer return **(number 4),** and issue the credit so we can get it off our books, and let the customer know the situation has been resolved.

Being able to effectively prioritize the types of tasks above goes a long way in developing solid time management skills. Remember, *"Organization and time management are the keys to business life."* The Customer Service Rep or Salesperson who can organize, plan, and manage his time will most likely be successful in today's hectic business pace.

**Let us look at one more real life example**. This is the type of scenario that can easily pop up at any time  An Inside Sales Rep is having a pretty productive day when out of the blue everything hits at once. **A**. A customer calls to expedite an order. **B**. While the Inside Sales Rep is on the phone with the customer a Sales Engineer brings out a rush order that has to get into the system so it can ship overnight to another customer. **C**. At the same time another Sales Engineer has to have a large dollar quote entered since the customer claimed they would make the purchase as soon as they received the quote. **D**. While all this is going on the Inside Sales Rep also remembers there are a number of reports that need reviewed by the end of the day. What does the Inside Sales Rep do? What would you do? How would you attack these tasks?

There really is not any right or wrong answer to this scenario. The key is to learn how to juggle and prioritize. This is what I would recommend in this situation:

1. **A**. We take care of the customer on the phone first. We can either get him his information right away if it is readily available or let him know we will get back to him in some efficient time frame. (Dynamic Step 1, Do what you say you are going to do). Obviously we are going to take care of our customer who is already on the phone.

2. **C**. We enter the quote into the system, print it off and fax or email it to the customer. We let the Sales Engineer know so he can follow up with the potential buyer right away.

3. **B**. We enter the rush order into the system and print the packing slip to ship it to the customer overnight to be on site the next morning.

4. **D**. Finally we finish reviewing the reports before the end of the day.

Obviously we will take care of the customer who is on the phone first. Question, why did we choose the quote over the rush order? Because the order is already business in house and even though it is important that we take care of it, the quote is **future business on the street**. The customer has told us as soon as he gets his pricing he will make the purchase. We need to wrap this up as soon as possible and get the business in house. After the quotation task is completed we will take care of the rush order so the customer receives his product in time to finish his job. We finish by filing the backlog at the end of the day. By prioritizing this way we have helped our customers and ourselves. Please remember the better service we provide the better we take care of our customer, our team, and ourselves.

The bottom line is you need to be able to multi-task, stay organized, prioritize and make things happen. Using your action plan and the prioritization method will keep you on track and on top of your workload. Once again, "***Organization and time management are the keys to business life***." Remember Dynamic Step 2 and stay organized and focused. ***Manage your time; don't let time manage you***.

# Dynamic Step 3: Ask questions, close the sale

If a customer calls us and we simply provide the information or product he requests are we really helping him meet his ultimate goal? Maybe, but there is probably more to his actual objective. By asking a few simple questions, we may find out what the customer's true goal is and we may have a way to help the customer to actually meet that goal. Sure, we can simply supply the product and go on our way. In fact, this is the path of least resistance and most CSR's are anxious to get on to the next task at hand because they usually have a very heavy work load, but the most successful Customer Service Reps will take the time to ask some of the following probing questions:

**1.) What are you going to do with this product?**

**2.) What is your goal?**

**3.) When are you going to put this in service?**

**4.) Do you need any help with the rest of your project?**

**5.) How else can I help you meet your goal?**

**6.) Is there anything else I can do for you today?**

Asking any of the above questions or others specific to your business may open other doors, help discover new opportunities, help identify and meet the customer's true goal and increase your business. It takes little time to ask these easy questions and the pay off can be substantial.

**The other part of Dynamic Step 3 is to ask for the business**.

Customer Service Reps (who focus on providing information and answers) and Inside Sales Associates (who are more likely to be involved in actual selling) work way too hard to not ask for the business on every call. For example: A customer calls up and asks you to jump through hoops and get his pricing and delivery to him immediately. You go into action:

1. **You make the appropriate calls.**
2. **You look up the pricing.**
3. **You check stock or delivery status.**
4. **You call the customer back and deliver the information in a timely and efficient manner**.

The customer states, "Thanks, I will let you know." Obviously you have put forth a great deal of time and effort to make this happen **and this is the time to ask for the business.** Remember, you get what you ask for in life. If you ask for the business chances are, based on the time and effort put in, you will close the deal.

Asking for the business will also help your customer. If we solidify the sale that is one less item on his daily task list and he is one step closer to achieving his goal. It may be as easy as saying, "By the way Mr. customer should I get that on order for you," or possibly the more direct approach, "What PO number should I put on that order?" **The bottom line is it is up to you to ask for business!** You deserve it and keep in mind you get what you ask for in life. Asking these questions will benefit both you and your customer. Remember the following closing questions:

**1.) What PO number should I put on your order?**

**2.) When did you need this on site?**

**3.) How many do you need me to ship?**

**4.) How should I ship your material?**

**5.) Do you need anything else with your shipment?**

**6.) Should I ship this regular way or do you need it sooner?**

**7.) Where should I ship your material?**

**8.) Do you want me to call you when this has shipped?**

**9.) Do you want me to call you with a tracking number?**

You will notice all nine questions are soft closes *(subtle questions or recommendations designed to encourage the customer to make the purchase)* that give the customer the opportunity to give you the sale and get this task off his desk. These soft closes can be used in any business environment. Your customer is just as busy as you and he needs your service.

Take the approach that you are removing a huge burden from his overloaded work schedule. We have now eliminated at least one task or project for him. We want to make it easy and beneficial for the customer to do business with us. Our main goal is to help the customer meet his goal and of course make money for our company and for us in doing so effectively.

**In Dynamic Step 3** we have found that by asking the right questions we will benefit both the customer and our company. Finding the customer's true and bottom line goal will go a long way in building our relationship. We have also learned that since we do provide a valuable service and good product we have every right to ask for the business and close the sale. Once again you probably won't get the business unless you go for the close. Closing the sale will benefit both you and your customer. Remember Dynamic Step 3. ***Ask questions, close the sale***.

# Dynamic Step 4: Know your business, know your product

As Customer Service Reps, Inside Sales Reps, or Sales Associates one may never become a technical or product guru, but it is imperative that we know our business and our product. As stated earlier in **Dynamic Step 1**, when the customer calls he wants to know two things. *1. That someone is on top of his situation and 2. That everything is going to work out and his goal will be met.*

It is up to us to know our business and **how** to get the answers to solve the customer's problem. To be a Dynamic Customer Service Rep we have to know how to make things happen. We also need to have a good understanding of our products so we know how to utilize them to help the customer achieve his goal. We may not be product experts, but we can "*walk the walk and talk the talk*." If your in Men's Fine Clothing Sales know your suits, if your in Intangible Sales know your investments and policies, if you are in Industrial Sales know your products and applications. If we make the customer feel good and confident about our abilities we will be able to build our working relationship. A big part of being a top CSR is to know **how, where, when, and from whom** to get good answers and information. Therefore; having a good relationship with your suppliers and vendors is essential to your ultimate success.

You want to be able to count on your contacts to help you the same way you help your customer. The more you work with your suppliers the more you will learn about the products and the business in general. Each week you should take home some type of product literature, catalogs, etc. to review or study the material on the vendor's website. **The more you know about your product lines the more confident you will come across with your customers**. Once again you don't have to be a product expert but you need to be very comfortable with your focus products. When your supplier Rep is in make sure you get a chance to discuss his product lines and general company information.

Along with a good understanding of your focus products I highly recommend you learn all the history, background, goals and other pertinent information about your company. Remember every time you speak to a customer over the phone or meet face to face you are representing your company, your product, (by knowing the features and benefits) and yourself. You should seek out any new information or exciting news about your company and your products.

**For example**:   While you are taking care of a customer's particular situation or goal, don't be afraid to mention any other products or aspects of your company that may help him in the future.  The more pertinent information you give that is relative to his future needs or goals the more likely he will come back to your for future opportunities. If you feel good and excited about your company and the products you have to offer then your customer will develop that same feeling and enthusiasm. If he feels like you have a good product to offer and the type of company that supports and stands behind the product he will be inclined to take advantage of the opportunities you present.

"*Relationship Selling*" is another big part of the equation. The customer wants to know that after the sale you won't disappear into thin air but will be there when he needs you again.  In fact, there is probably nothing more encouraging to a customer than to get a follow-up phone call asking about the product or the end result of his project.  Think about your own customer service situations. When was the last time a customer service person followed up with you after the sale? How did that make you feel?

Let's take for example a new customer to whom we sold a small dollar item that he needed quickly. That could be the end of the story, but let's say we follow up with a phone call the next day to the customer making sure he received his product and that it took care of his needs. We then ask if there is anything else we can do to help him finish his project or achieve his goal. This is *"Relationship Selling!"* This is going beyond just getting the sale. We are now developing the business relationship.

By following through on your sale and being personally involved in your customer's success he will understand that you are in his corner for the long haul and not just trying to collect sales. This goes back to the concept of truly helping the customer achieve his goal or objective.

By *"relationship selling"* your product, your company, and yourself with confidence and enthusiasm you will secure your customer's long-term commitment to grow your business partnership. You will also build your confidence and your overall customer service skills. Remember Dynamic Step 4. **_Know your business, know your product._**

# Dynamic Step 5: Do whatever it takes to get the job done

This final step may be the most crucial of all and the one that brings everything together. If we work on **Dynamic Steps 1- 4** but don't go the distance in **Dynamic Step 5,** then we will never fully reach our full customer service potential. We must be willing to finish everything we do with **Dynamic Step 5** to reach our goal. This final step will help us provide Dynamic Customer Service.

In today's business world you will never be truly successful by watching the clock, being ready to bolt out the door at 5:00PM, or by taking the path of least resistance. It is essential to be able to complete tasks and projects in a timely and efficient manner. It is also imperative to satisfy the customer at every opportunity. Finally you must learn to work outside your circle, outside your zone, and rid yourself of any tunnel vision. This means attacking and jumping into areas or situations that may be new or uncomfortable for you. The more you expand your horizons the more of an asset you will be to your customer and your company.

Let us say for example that your responsibility is to work with three particular vendor lines and products. A customer calls looking for information about a different vendor product and the CSR that handles that line is away from his desk. You could say that he is out and that he will call back as soon as possible, but why not take the call and see if you can help. If nothing else you can gather all the information and get the response process started. This will help your team member and imagine what it will mean to your customer. The customer will realize that he can call on anyone on your team and he will get answers or resolutions. **Again, the more informed and prepared you are the more valuable you will be to your customers and to your company.**

Take a hard look at the team members who are the top performers in your company. The people who move up the corporate ladder, make the most money, and truly enjoy job satisfaction. Do they really have more skills, know how or true talent than others? More than likely they are the team members who are willing to go the distance and somehow always seem to make things happen and get the job done no matter what the circumstances.

I believe you will find they are using some method of the five easy steps we have been discussing whether they realize it or not. They are organized, confident, know their product and their company, they always ask for the business, and they do what they say they are going to do **(remember the Dynamic 5 steps).** I have personally been successful in the three different areas of my career, Industrial Distribution, Investment Sales, and Retail Business because I effectively implemented these five steps and I have always been willing to **go the distance to get the job done!**

I have spent much of my career doing recruiting, interviewing, and hiring and when all is said and done the candidate who I normally hire is one I know will do whatever it takes do get the job done. Companies who fill positions with committed team players who are proactive, good organizers, efficient time managers, and have confidence in their products; their company and themselves are most likely to be successful. Much of a company's success is dependent upon how they build their nucleus and their overall team.

To become this type of team player you should walk through the office door in the morning with confidence and a great game plan for your day. You should be ready to focus on business for the next eight plus hours or so and be as productive as possible. Go right to your action plan you set-up the night before and begin with the first task. As you go through your day cross off the tasks that are accomplished and keep moving forward. Remember, "**Organization and time management are the keys to business life**." Do not waste time or energy. Don't get me wrong, you can take a break or breather, chat for a couple of minutes with co-workers, etc., but you should be very focused on your business and the tasks at hand throughout the day.

Follow your game plan and find a way to make things happen. When problems or emergencies arise attack them head on and focus on ideas and solutions. Always be willing to go the distance and give the extra ten percent. And when things start to get overwhelming take a deep breath, and figure out your next move. Finally throw out the phrases "**that's not my job**" and/or "**I can't get that done**." Your mindset and attitude must be "**let me see what I can do**" and "**somehow I will make this happen**."

If you go to work with this attitude and commitment you will be amazed at just how much you will accomplish. Obviously this makes you feel great and puts you in a position of strength on your team or within your company. **When the going gets tough the tough get going**. Always remember Dynamic Step 5. *Do whatever it takes to get the job done!*

# Summary

We have just discussed the five steps to achieving dynamic customer service and more. As stated before these steps come from over twenty years of meeting customer service goals and objectives. By following these five steps on a daily basis you will begin to achieve the kind of customer service approach that will benefit both you and your company. First and foremost, "*Organization and time management are the keys to business life.*"

By reading this book you have found that we are not discussing rocket science or brain surgery but good common sense approaches in dealing with your customers combined with a proactive and get the job done attitude. This is what customer service is all about. Think about the times you have felt you received good service in one form or another. It normally entails the concepts we have just discussed.

The key now is to take these five dynamic steps and implement them in your daily business approach. Reading this book was a good first step to customer service success, but like anything else that works successfully you must take the concepts discussed in this book and put them into play in your environment. It will also take some time to fine tune some of the material discussed but by applying the basic foundations you will start to see positive results. By implementing these easy five steps you will develop a Dynamic Customer Service approach to your business and more! Let's review the steps one last time.

**Dynamic Step 1**: *Do what you say you are going to do.* If you commit to something for your customer, team member, or employee then figure out a way to make it happen. This will build trust and lay the foundation for a solid working relationship.

**Dynamic Step 2**: *Time Management and Organization.* If you are well organized and you can juggle tasks, prioritize, and manage your time chances are you will be successful. Remember the two keys. Start each day with a solid action plan to follow and prioritize your workload accordingly. One last time, "*Organization and time management are the keys to business life*!"

**Dynamic Step 3**: *Ask questions; close the sale.* Always remember to ask the easy questions we discussed to find the customer's true goal or hot button. Remember just selling the product doesn't necessarily mean we completed the goal. We need to get to the root of the goal or objective. Also, you put a lot of time and effort into helping your customers; therefore, ask for the business and close the sale. The customer expects it. He knows you are in the business to make money and if you deliver good product, quality service, and stand behind your product and company then he expects to pay for this process.

**Dynamic Step 4**: *Know your business; know your product*. This is the one step in which you need to be very well read and prepared. Along with the four pro-active and common based steps you will need to be very solid on your product lines and how to get related answers and information quickly. You also need to be very well versed on your company history, goals, and business approach. Remember, you are always selling your product, your company, and yourself.

**Dynamic Step 5**: *Do whatever it takes to get the job done*. This is the step that brings all the rest together and puts the icing on the cake. You must be willing to go the distance, give the extra ten percent, go above and beyond the call of duty, and figure out a way regardless of the situation or crisis to make things happen, get the job done, and meet your customer's goals and objectives.

The rest is up to you.  Please take these five steps to heart and implement them into your daily business plan.  They will have a lasting positive effect on your customer service career and on your team.  They will help you move to the top of your game in providing Dynamic Customer Service.  As you well know by now the title of this work is "**Dynamore!  5 Steps to Dynamic Customer Service and More."**  What is the **More**? More is going above and beyond the call of duty.  More is asking questions, closing business, following up with customers, and helping your team members.  More is doing whatever it takes to get the job done regardless of the situation.  More is meeting your customer's goals and objectives.  More is helping your company grow by providing quality customer service.  More is everything you do that is one step beyond what is required. More is what it takes to truly provide Dynamic Customer Service!

By the way, have you figured out the true meaning of customer service?  It's actually very simple.  Customer service means different things to different customers, but to sum it all up, "***true customer service is what the customer really needs from us to help achieve his goal or objective***." That's the bottom line!  Use these dynamic steps to achieve the goal!

Good luck in everything you do.  Go the distance for your customer, your company, and yourself.  Remember the five steps because **Dynamic Customer Service** will truly make the difference!

# About the Author

David R. Post was born and raised in the small town of Claysville, Pennsylvania. He still resides today in neighboring West Alexander, Pennsylvania with his wife Launa Haney Post. Mr. Post has over twenty years of customer service, sales, and business operations experience in the Retail, Investment Sales, and Industrial Distribution business sectors. He has held the positions of Sales Specialist, Inside Sales, Customer Service Manager, Operations Manager, Director of Operations, and Vice President of Operations. He also is co-founder and President of a private operational business consulting firm. Mr. Post has dedicated his career to enhancing the service and daily business operations of small businesses and larger corporate entities using the five steps to Dynamic Customer Service.

www.ingramcontent.com/pod-product-compliance
Lightning Source LLC
Chambersburg PA
CBHW021922170526
45157CB00005B/2138